ANCIENT GREECE

BY DANIEL R. FAUST

Gareth Stevens
PUBLISHING

CRASH COURSE

Please visit our website, www.garethstevens.com. For a free color catalog of all our high-quality books, call toll free 1-800-542-2595 or fax 1-877-542-2596.

Cataloging-in-Publication Data

Names: Faust, Daniel R.
Title: Ancient Greece / Daniel R. Faust.
Description: New York : Gareth Stevens Publishing, 2019. | Series: A look at ancient civilizations | Includes glossary and index.
Identifiers: ISBN 9781538231548 (pbk.) | ISBN 9781538230060 (library bound) | ISBN 9781538233245 (6 pack)
Subjects: LCSH: Greece--Civilization--To 146 B.C.--Juvenile literature. | Greece--History--To 146 B.C.--Juvenile literature.
Classification: LCC DF77.F38 2019 | DDC 938--dc23

First Edition

Published in 2019 by
Gareth Stevens Publishing
111 East 14th Street, Suite 349
New York, NY 10003

Copyright © 2019 Gareth Stevens Publishing

Designer: Reann Nye
Editor: Tayler Cole

Photo credits: Series art (writing background) mcherevan/Shutterstock.com, (map) Andrey_Kuzmin/Shutterstock.com; cover, p. 1 anyaivanova/Shutterstock.com; p. 5 Samot/Shutterstock.com; p. 7 dikobraziy/Shutterstock.com; p. 9 Georgy Markov/Shutterstock.com; p. 11 f8grapher/Shutterstock.com; p. 13 Alex Tihonovs/Shutterstock.com; p. 15 Sven Hansche/Shutterstock.com; p. 17 Nastasic/DigitalVision Vectors/Getty Images; p. 19 Haris vythoulkas/Shutterstock.com; p. 21 Denis Kornilov/Shutterstock.com; p. 23 Coupe attribuée au Peintre de Triptolème./Alonso de Mendoza/Wikipedia.org; p. 25 Universal History Archive/Universal Images Group/Getty Images; p. 27 Walter Bibikow/AWL Images/Getty Images; p. 29 cge2010/Shutterstock.com.

Printed in the United States of America

CPSIA compliance information: Batch #CW19GS: For further information contact Gareth Stevens, New York, New York at 1-800-542-2595.

CONTENTS

Words in the glossary appear in **bold** type the first time they are used in the text.

MOUNTAINS AND ISLANDS

Greece is a country of many mountains and islands located on the Mediterranean Sea. There isn't a lot of good farmland, so most ancient Greeks lived along the coastline and became fishermen or traders. They also raised sheep, goats, and pigs along the mountainsides.

4

Make The Grade

Around 3000 BC, the first European civilization rose near
the Aegean Sea in what is today the country of Greece.

5

THE MINOANS AND MYCENAEANS

The first powerful civilization to rise around the Aegean Sea was that of the Minoans on the island of Crete. The Minoans were seafaring traders with a powerful navy. Around 1500 BC, the Mycenaean civilization rose on the Greek mainland. The Mycenaeans **conquered** the Minoans around 1400 BC.

Aegean Sea

Greece
Mycenaean civilization

Crete
Minoan civilization

Mediterranean Sea

Make The Grade

The Mycenaean language is the oldest known form
of the Greek language.

THE RISE OF CITY-STATES

The Mycenaean civilization fell around 1200 BC. From then until about 900 BC, Greece entered a time some historians call the Dark Age. This is because the population decreased and the Greek civilization broke into many small, separate cities.

Make The Grade

Greece's Dark Age is sometimes called the Homeric Age. Homer was a Greek poet who wrote about the **mythical** Trojan War between the Greeks and the people of Troy.

9

By about 800 BC, city-states began to rise in Greece. A city-state, called a *polis* by the Greeks, was a city that controlled nearby farms and villages. City-states were independent, which meant they ruled themselves instead of being ruled by a single king or **emperor**.

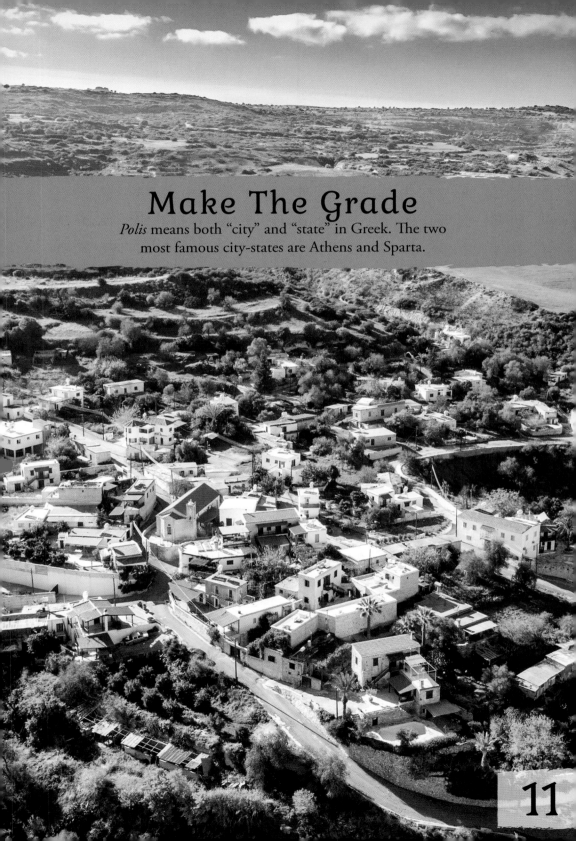

Make The Grade

Polis means both "city" and "state" in Greek. The two most famous city-states are Athens and Sparta.

GREEK COLONIZATION

Around 700 BC, the Greeks began **colonizing** around the Mediterranean Sea. They were looking for new people to trade with and were curious about the rest of the world. Their new colonies helped spread Greek culture, or ways of life, to other parts of the world.

Make The Grade

By 500 BC Greece had around 500 colonies in places
such as modern-day Italy, France, Spain, North Africa,
and around the Adriatic and Black Seas.

13

ANCIENT ATHENS

In the 400s BC, Athens was the largest and the most important city-state, known for its art, **philosophy**, and poetry. Several great thinkers and poets lived and worked in Athens. The Parthenon, one of the greatest **temples** in Greece, was built at the top of the city.

Make The Grade

Athens was also known for its **court** system. A group
of people called a jury would hear both sides of an
argument before deciding who was to blame.

15

THE BIRTH OF DEMOCRACY

The word "**democracy**" comes from the Greek word *demos*, which means "citizens" or "the people." Greek city-states weren't ruled by a single person. In most city-states, all the male citizens were allowed to participate, or take part, in running the government.

Make The Grade

Women, slaves, and people originally from other countries weren't considered citizens in ancient Greece.

GODS AND HEROES

The Greeks believed in a pantheon, or group, of gods and goddesses. These gods were a way for the ancient Greeks to understand and explain the natural world around them. Most gods were believed to live in temples where the Greeks would go to **worship** them.

Make The Grade

The most important gods in Greek religion were the
Olympian gods. They lived on Mount Olympus and were
led by Zeus, the greatest of them all.

LET THE GAMES BEGIN

The first Olympics were a series of sporting events held in honor of Zeus, king of the Greek gods. They likely began around 776 BC and were held every 4 years for about 400 years. People from city-states across the Greek world took part in the Olympics.

Make The Grade

Some unmarried women were allowed to take part in their own kind of Olympics. These games were called the Heraia, in honor of Zeus's wife Hera.

21

TIMES OF WAR

Beginning in 490 BC, the Persian Empire tried to take over Greece. In order to win, the Greeks often fought in a tight line called a phalanx (FAY-lankz) in which they used their **shields** to protect each other. The Greeks won the Persian War in 479 BC.

Make The Grade

Athens and Sparta, the two most powerful city-states in Greece, fought together during the Persian War.

After the Persian War, Athens became very powerful. War broke out between Athens and Sparta. The Peloponnesian War started around 431 BC and lasted almost 30 years. Sparta finally defeated Athens in 404 BC and became the most powerful city-state in ancient Greece.

Make The Grade

The Peloponnesian War gets its name from Peloponneus, the area of
Greece in the Mediterranean Sea where Sparta is located.

ALEXANDER THE GREAT

Philip II was the king of Macedon, a kingdom north of Greece. In 338 BC, he conquered Greece and united, or brought together, almost all of the Greek city-states. By 323 BC, Philip II's son, Alexander the Great, had **expanded** this empire to include Egypt, Persia, and India.

Make The Grade

Alexander the Great's empire helped spread the Greek
culture all across the ancient world.

LASTING INFLUENCE

Many buildings from ancient Greece have survived to the modern day. Many of these buildings are temples. Greek styles still **influence** artists and builders. Columns like those found on the Parthenon in Athens can be seen in buildings such as the Lincoln Memorial in Washington, DC.

column

Make The Grade

Many famous artists, such as Michelangelo, copied the styles of ancient Greek **statues**. Their art continued to spread the influence of Greek culture around Europe.

TIMELINE OF ANCIENT GREECE

c. 3000–1400 BC
The Minoans rule the
Mediterranean Sea.

c. 1500–1200 BC
The Mycenaeans control
mainland Greece.

c. 1200–c. 900 BC
Greece enters
the Dark Age.

776 BC
The first Olympics
are held.

c. 500 BC
Athens begins to grow into
the largest city-state.

490–479 BC
Greece is invaded twice
by the Persians before
defeating them in the
Persian War.

431–404 BC
The Peloponnesian War
is fought between
Athens and Sparta.

338 BC
Philip II of Macedon
conquers Greece.

GLOSSARY

colonize: to establish a colony, or a piece of land under the control of another country

conquer: to take by force

court: a legal meeting in which facts about crimes or disagreements are presented to a judge and jury so that decisions can be made according to the law

democracy: the free and equal right of every person to participate in a government

emperor: the ruler of an empire, which is a large area of land under the control of a single ruler

expand: to make larger

influence: to have an effect on

mythical: like a legend or story

philosophy: a system of thought made to try to understand the nature of that which is real

shield: a piece of metal or wood used to guard the body in battle

statue: a figure usually of a person or animal that is made from stone or metal

temple: a building for worship

worship: to honor as a god

FOR MORE INFORMATION

BOOKS

Edwards, Roberta. *Where Is The Parthenon?* New York, NY: Grosset & Dunlap, 2016.

Yasuda, Anita. *Explore Ancient Greece*. Mankato, MN: 12 Story Library, 2018.

WEBSITE

Ancient Greece

www.bbc.co.uk/education/topics/z87tn39

Learn more about what family life, mythology, war, and art were like in ancient Greece.

INDEX